Complete

Conduct Principles

for the

21st Century

Complete

Conduct Principles

for the

21st Century

John Newton, Ph.D.

Nicer Century World Publishing

Somerville, Massachusetts

#42810892

Published by

Nicer Century World Publishing, Somerville, Massachusetts, USA

Manufactured in the United States of America by BookMasters, Inc.

10 9 8 7 6 5 4 3 2 1

Library of Congress Cataloging-in-Publication Data

Newton, John, date.
  Complete conduct principles for the 21st century / John Newton.
    p. cm.
  Includes index.
  ISBN 0-9673705-7-4 (alk. paper) – ISBN 0-9673705-8-2 (pbk. : alk. paper)
    1. Conduct of life. I. Title.

BJ1581.2 .N49 2000
170'.44–dc21

                      99-057919
                    LC-CIP

ISBN 0967370574 (hardcover)
ISBN 0967370582 (paperback)

Attention schools and organizations:
Quantity discounts are available on bulk purchases of this book. For information contact
the publisher or the distributor, BookMasters,Inc., P.O. Box 388, Ashland, OH 44805,
FAX: 419-281-6883, e-mail: order@bookmaster.com

About the Author

John Newton holds a Ph.D. from MIT, and does researches at Harvard. His long-term research on *the personal conduct in the human society of the 21st century* results in this book.

To the Memory of My Mother,

the greatest mother in my mind.

PREFACE

This is *not* a religious book, *nor* is a collection of old conduct rules. This handbook of complete conduct principles for the *21st* century results from a long-term research and thinking. This research used not only ethics, philosophy and the humanities but also science, sociology, medicine and psychology. This thinking was built not only upon sentiment and love but also upon rationality and logic.

Science and technology will be more advanced in the *21st* century than ever. During the 20th century the inventions of traffic instruments, such as cars, planes, etc., and of communication tools, such as telephone, FAX, e-mail, Internet, etc., have shortened the "distances" among people. In the *21st* century further advanced science and technology will make traffic instruments and communication tools much better than in the 20th century, so that the "distances" among people will be further shortened. On the other hand, the protection and respect for privacy and "personal space" will be greater than ever, so that the "distances" among people will be increased.

Primarily due to economic factors and secondly due to social ones, the structure unit of mankind gradually evolved from a grand kin complex in the agriculture era to a big family, a small family, ...; in the *21st* century it will further approach an individual system. The support to an individual from his or her family as it was in the past will be weaker, and one will be supposed to further rely on oneself, not only regarding finances and living but also regarding conduct and managements. On the other hand, the growing independence of life and work will make a lot of people lonelier and more desirous of friendships — hoping to get comforts, encouragements or other spiritual supports.

The desire for personal freedom will be stronger

than ever. On the other hand, the law in the *21st* century will tend to be further detailed and complicated, and will make more limits and constraints to many kinds of personal freedom. The law of sexual harassment is an example. In the *21st* century the problem of sexual harassment will continue to bluster in the US, and that hurricane will also sweep other countries; a lot of nations and regions will adopt various laws of sexual harassment.

The advance of science and technology, the improvement of traffic instruments and communication tools, the promotion of the knowledge and wisdom of mankind, and the rise of the sense of internationalization and the sense of the world make the "boundaries" between nations gradually faded, and cause the customs, cultures and moral views to gradually approach internationalization. In the *21st* century this approach will be much more significant than ever.

These are a few examples of the society trends in the *21st* century. These trends will cause the properties of contradiction, complication, multi-direction, multi-layer, multi-dimension and multi-culture inter-blending of the human society to be much stronger in the *21st* century than ever. Facing such a new society, we have a new challenge: *What is good conduct in the 21st century?* We need a new thinking and research.

Computing the average of all dimensions of the whole society, we know that the social order & moral senses and people's psychology, minds, souls & spirits in the latter half of the 20th century went significantly in the *negative* direction. If we do not turn them and go to the rescue in time, in the *21st* century mankind will undergo a grievous disaster.

This problem reminds us that learning good conduct will be very important to the healthy development of the human society in the *21st* century. This will seriously affect mankind's happiness and destiny.

The rates of crimes, suicide, drug abuses, mental illnesses, ..., etc. have greatly increased for the past several decades (neglecting small fluctuations), particularly among youth. Recently school violence has made many pieces of nation-shaking highlighted headline news, which have already astounded the Americans. Some experts believe this is the most important national crisis the US is facing. Research shows that gun control and school security actions, the ways governments and schools are taking, can not solve the problem; worse, they may increase the resistant minds of some students. A proper and effective way to solve the problem is appropriate conduct education.

These problems further remind us that from now on learning good conduct should be placed as *No. 1* in education.

In the *21st* century all problems stated above will happen not only continuously in the US but also in lots of other countries all over the world, if we do not act.

While I was finishing writing this book, the US

President Bill Clinton's affair significantly raised the interest of the people all over the world as well as in the US in the questions: What is good conduct? What is bad conduct?

One of the main purposes of this book is to help solve all important problems discussed above. This book also wishes to help every individual solve his or her own conduct problems; good personal conduct is a basis for the good health of society.

In the *21st* century people will be generally too busy to patiently read and digest a whole serious book. Therefore, in order to provide most people with more useful help regarding conduct, a simple, easy, clear, convenient, self-contained and small handbook is more appropriate. This book is just so designed as to suit most people.

This is a handbook; it is not necessary for you to read through the whole book in one sitting. A later section is not based upon an earlier one. If in a section referring to other one(s) is needed, it will be indicated there. When a conduct problem or an interest in it develops, look over the *Contents* and look for one or a few principles closest to what you need. If you remember or guess a principle title, you may first look up its item number in the *Principle Index* at the end of the book and then look up its page number in the *Contents*. You may also use the *General Index* for the page number(s) of a specific subject. Read the explanation or discussion of each principle you wish to do, think, comprehend and digest it, and apply the principle(s) to your problem. In the course of time you will be familiar with all principles, and then, I hope, you will be able to approach the state that you can feel free to do whatever you like without violating any conduct principle.

There are 121 principles in all. They contain all needful basic conduct principles for the *21st* century. Each principle item has an explanation or discussion, generally brief, simple, easy, concise and clear; only a few need longer explanations and/or discussions.

For most adults and high-school students, this book is self-contained; it is (mostly) unnecessary to refer to other books or materials in order to understand this book. This saves your time and efforts, so that you can get what you need quickly and efficiently.

This book is a result of my long-term thinking and research. Now, on the eve of the *21st* century, I publish it in order to make a contribution to people in time.

In addition to my own thoughts and acquirements, this book also includes the best conduct minds, souls and spirits in both the Eastern and the Western cultures, different from each other; a fine and careful blend of those also produces some other novel results. This best suits the highly internationalized and multi-culture inter-blended society in the *21st* century, and may also help solve the problems the Western culture can not.

These 121 conduct principles cover not only what we should do but also what we should not do — especially aiming at the faults people make often and easily.

You probably have been familiar with some of the 121 principles, but not all. Even if you are familiar with all (or most), you probably may still violate some on occasion.

If you have ever violated any conduct principles in the past, just let it pass away. From now on you may have new conduct.

These 121 items are principles, not strict rules. It is indeed not easy to 100% abide by all of them all one's life. If you occasionally, having no other choices under some circumstances, slightly violate a principle without resulting in a remediless consequence, do not feel guilty too much. Refer to the relevant principles and their explanations or discussions in this book, examine the fault you made, and avoid doing it again.

This book is for your reference. It is unnecessary for you to agree on all contents. If you disagree on one portion of the contents, you probably can find many other ones nevertheless very useful to yourself. You may deduce other conduct rules from these principles, explanations and discussions, and particularly apply them to the special cases you encounter.

The partial overlaps among principles are unavoidable. The main reason is that the conduct principles are *inherently* partially overlapped. For the sake of the character of a handbook, in this book two principles may be separated and placed into two different items even if they have a partial overlap; often a reader of this handbook may wish to read at a time only the principle closest to what he or she needs then.

On the other hand, the partial overlaps among principles also have the following consequence. If you think there are any conduct principles not covered by this book, then they probably can be deduced from or implied by some of the 121 principles. Hence, although this book has only 121 principles, it should be complete for good conduct in the *21st* century; if you are able to well deduce other conduct rules from these 121 principles and also well apply them, the 121 principles should be sufficient for all you need for good conduct in the *21st* century.

In the explanations or discussions of many items I suggest referring to some other relevant ones. Such cross-references can make effects better. However the suggestion signs for the cross-references are necessarily incomplete; particularly because what a reader needs varies with person and case and, as stated above, conduct principles are inherently partially overlapped. I thus do not try to make such signs complete. If you wish to see all of what you need, it should be better to look for them with the methods suggested in the *How to Use This Handbook.*

This book is intended for people of almost all ages, from pre-teenagers to oldsters, regardless of the occupations, ranks, status, nationalities and regions. As for pre-teenagers, the effects can increase if they are helped by parents or teachers.

Except the issue of sexual harassment, this book does not discuss specifically the problems special to the treatments, dealings and associations between man and woman, including, for example, the marriage problems. For many of those problems, the customary factors are greater than the moral ones; they often vary with time and place, and the solutions often vary with case. The discussion on those problems should be placed in another book specializing in that subject. Moreover, this book has young readers, so that, except the problem of sexual harassment, discussing those topics is further inappropriate. This book is for *general* personal conduct principles, it is intended for both man and woman, and its content is mostly independent of gender. The special problems discussed above will change relatively rapidly with time; some existing in the 20th century and/or earlier (not including that of sexual harassment) will be gradually waning in the *21st* century, while new ones will rise. No matter how inconceivably those problems develop, most of the general personal conduct principles in this book will remain well applicable throughout the *21st* century, regardless of the gender(s) of the person(s) with whom you deal or associate.

In order to be concise, a principle title may be an adjective (omitting "Be") unless a principle title of verb or noun is placed in the same item.

In the following let's talk about some other benefits of good conduct.

First of all, good conduct is advantageous to work, job and career. This is a very obvious benefit and has been known to lots of people, so needs no more explanation here.

As for students, learning good conduct now will benefit future careers as well as school lives.

Good conduct may bring pleasures and happinesses to yourself, family, relatives, friends, people around, people you contact, and more.

If one seeks only for material enjoyment all one's life, won't it be pitiable as to one of the human beings very superior to all the other animals? A lot of conduct principles in this book may enhance the meaning of human life.

What I need to explain more is the relation between conduct and health.

Recently science shows that one's thought, emotion and behavior significantly affect one's health. Thought, emotion and behavior affect one another, and they can stimulate the brain, in consequence producing some substances and messages, significantly affecting a person's health; for example, affecting your immune system and healing function.

I would like to remind readers that thought, emotion and behavior are just the important ingredients of conduct. Hence you can realize that conduct and health have a deep relationship.

As one can know from the above, the discussion here on the relation between conduct and health not only is philosophy (in the narrow sense) but has a scientific basis.

If you follow the conduct principles in this book so that in the *21st* century you will have nicer and kinder behavior, stabler and pleasanter emotions, and more mature and wiser thoughts, then this will certainly benefit your health; the contrary situation may hurt health.

In addition to your own health, as discussed above, your good conduct may bring other people pleasures and happinesses so that it may benefit others' health; it benefits others as well as yourself.

In other words, your good conduct will benefit the minds, spirits and health both of yourself and of people around you.

The last several paragraphs discussed many benefits of good conduct. However, after this I wish to emphasize a point, the most important one, that, whatever benefits they are, we should have good conduct because each of us is a man, a member of the human society.

Many people are often moved to sigh that "the way of the world is daily getting worse" and "the world is declining in its moral values". Let's work together to make the *21st* century nicer than ever before!

I especially thank my wife, also a senior scholar, for her enthusiastic assistance all the way of achieving this book.

John Newton

Cambridge, Massachusetts
December 1998

CONTENTS

Preface 1

Contents 17

How to Use This Handbook 27

A Few Explanations and Pieces of Advice

regarding Using This Handbook 29

1. Honest 35

2. Sincere; 36

    Cordial

3. Keep Faith; 37

    Keep Your Promises;

    Keep Your Words;

    Be Careful in Making a Promise;

    Lay Emphasis on Faith and on Promise

4. Humble 39

5. Respect Other People 40

6. Upright; 41

    Righteous

7. Tolerant 42

8. Help Other People 43

9. Respect Other Person's Privacy 44

10. Keep an Appropriate Distance 45

11. Sympathy; 47

Compassion

12. Humor 48

13. Good Manners 49

14. Fine *Chih-Jyr*; 50

that is, Fine Outward Manifestation of Tempera-

ment and Disposition

15. Appreciating and Rewarding Your Parents; 51

Filial Piety

16. Incorruptness 52

17. Fair; 53

Just

18. Understand Yourself 54

19. Self-respect; 55

Self-confidence;

Elimination of the Sense of Inferiority

20. Try to Understand Other Person; 57

Avoid Misunderstanding

21. Don't Overestimate or Underestimate a Friendship Too Much 58

22. When You Use a Modern Communication Tool, Unless Necessary, Don't Expect an Excessively Quick Response from a Friend 59

23. Your Expectation Should Not Exceed the Reality Too Much 63

24. Be Considerate to Others; 64
Think from Other Person's Point of View

25. Guess Other Person's Feelings by Your Own; 65
Place Yourself in Another's Place

26. Don't Build Your Joy upon Other Person's Pain 66

27. Enjoy Freedom but Don't Disturb Other People 67

28. Being *Houh-Dau*; 68
that is, Blend of Being Kindhearted, Being Generous, Being Honest and Being Considerate

29. Propriety; 69
Courtesy

30. Kind 69

31. Generous 70

32. Harmonious 70

33. Do As Other People Like under Some Circum-

stances 71

34. Distinguish Clearly between Right and Wrong &

between Good and Evil 72

35. Moral Sense 73

36. Sense of Honor 74

37. Sense of Shame 75

38. Sense of Responsibility 76

39. *Yih-Chi*; 77

that is, Blend of Faith, Righteousness, Being Care-

ful of Friendships, Being Faithful to Friends, and

Appreciation & Reward for Favors

40. Don't Be Meddlesome 79

41. Don't Transfer Anger from One Matter/Person to

Another 80

42. Don't Act Only According to Your Emotions with-

out Restraint 82

43. Don't Cause People Around Pains or Unpleasant-

nesses 83

44. Ethics of Competitions 84

45. Avoid Being Jealous of Other Person . . . 85

46. Avoid That Other Person Is Jealous of You   86

47. Don't Rely on the Competitor's Fall but on Your

Own Rise for a Competition 87

48. Never Do Harm to Other Person 88

49. Love; 88

Benevolence;

Mercy;

Charity;

Humanity;

Virtue

50. Broad Love 89

51. Steady 89

52. Careful in Speaking 90

53. Never Be Impulsive; 91

Never Lose Self-control

54. Calm 93

55. Bearing 94

56. Rational 95

57. Talk Reason 96

58. Broad-minded 97

59. Don't Speak Ill of Others 97

60. Avoid Criticizing a Third Person 98

61. True 99

62. Optimistic 100

63. Courageous; 101

Firm, Unyielding and Strong

64. Independence; 102

Unless Necessary, Don't Depend on Other People

65. Open-minded 105

66. Straightforward 105

67. Resolute 106

68. Action Is Better Than Speaking in Some Cases 106

69. Don't Boast of Yourself; 107

Don't Brag of Yourself;

Don't Exaggerate;

Don't Talk Recklessly;

Don't Invent False Information

70. Unless Necessary, Talk Less about Yourself but

Concern Yourself More about Other People 108

71. Self-examination 109

72. Have the Courage to Acknowledge a Fault; 110

Correct It When You Know a Fault

73. Magnanimous to Others; 111

Lenient to Others

74. Don't Take Advantage of Other Person's Weak-

ness 112

75. Don't Use a Friend 112

76. Careful about Your Style of Conversation . 113

77. Careful about Your Behavior 114

78. Careful about Your Habits of Cleanliness and Hy-

giene 115

79. Develop Your Habits of Proper and Refined Behav-

ior 116

80. Don't Make an Arbitrary Implication . . . 117

81. Objective 119

82. Creditable; 120

Trustworthy

83. Showing Morality Is More Important Than Show-

ing Cleverness 121

84. Don't Make Mischiefs and Troubles among

People 122

85. Don't Bother about the Trifles of the Unworthy

Affairs of Relations among People; 123

Don't Bother about Other Person's Incorrect Criticism

86. Avoid Generating Enemies 124

87. You Would Rather Be Owed by Other Person Than Owe Him/Her 124

88. Try to Interest Yourself in Another's Talk during a Friendly or Social Conversation 125

89. During a Social Conversation with Several Persons, Try to Take Care of All 126

90. Don't Curse or Grumble Arbitrarily . . . 127

91. Consultation and Mutual Consent 128

92. Friendly 129

93. Warm 129

94. Concern Yourself about Other People . . . 130

95. Don't Judge a Person by His or Her Outward Appearance 131

96. Don't Criticize or Tease Another's Outward Appearance 132

97. Acknowledgment 133

98. Patient 134

99. Keep Your Appointments on Time 134

100. Help Relieve Friends' Worries; 135

Share Your Joy with Friends;

Congratulate or Praise Friends

101. Help Friends but Don't Intend to Gain Any Profit

or Advantage from a Friend 136

102. If You Want to Do a Thing, Do It Well . . 137

103. Lasting 138

104. Don't Discriminate against One According to

One's Disability 138

105. Don't Discriminate against One According to

One's Race or Color 139

106. Don't Discriminate against One According to

One's Nationality or National Origin . . . 140

107. Don't Discriminate against One According to

One's State Residence, Region or Accent . 142

108. Don't Discriminate against One According to

One's Gender 145

109. Don't Discriminate against One According to

One's Outward Appearance 146

110. Don't Discriminate against One According to

One's Poverty 147

111. Don't Discriminate against One According to

One's Religion Choice 148

112. Democracy 149

113. Sense of Public Morality 149

114. Don't Let Your Sayings and Doings Transgress

What Is Proper 150

115. Be Careful! Don't Make a Sexual Harassment 151

116. Law-abiding 154

117. View of the International Society 156

118. View of Peace 157

119. View of the World 158

120. View of *Dah-Turng* in the *21st* Century; . 160

that is, Blended View of Universal Harmony, a Nice

Human Society, and Sharing the World with All

People

121. Consistent 161

Principle Index 163

General Index 175

How to Use This Handbook

This is a handbook; it is not necessary for you to read through the whole book in one sitting. A later section is not based upon an earlier one. If in a section referring to other one(s) is needed, it will be indicated there.

When a conduct problem or an interest in it develops, look over the *Contents* and look for one or a few principles closest to what you need. If you remember or guess a principle title, you may first look up its item number in the *Principle Index* at the end of the book and then look up its page number in the *Contents*. You may also use the *General Index* for the page number(s) of a specific subject.

Read the explanation or discussion of each principle you wish to do, think, comprehend and digest it, and apply the principle(s) to your problem.

In the course of time you will be familiar with all principles, and then, I hope, you will be able to approach the state that you can feel free to do whatever you like without violating any conduct principle.

A Few Explanations
and Pieces of Advice
regarding
Using This Handbook

In the *21st* century people will be generally too busy to patiently read and digest a whole serious book. Therefore, in order to provide most people with more useful help regarding conduct, a simple, easy, clear, convenient, self-contained and small handbook is more appropriate. This book is just so designed as to suit most people.

There are 121 principles in all. They contain all needful basic conduct principles for the *21st* century. Each principle item has an explanation or discussion, generally brief, simple, easy, concise and clear; only a few need longer explanations and/or discussions.

For most adults and high-school students, this book is self-contained; it is (mostly) unnecessary to refer to other books or materials in order to understand this book. This saves your time and efforts, so that you can get what you need quickly and efficiently.

In addition to my own thoughts and acquirements, this book also includes the best conduct minds, souls and spirits in both the Eastern and the Western cultures, different from each other; a fine and careful blend of those also produces some other novel results. This best suits the highly internationalized and multi-culture inter-blended society in the *21st* century, and may also help solve the problems the Western culture can not.

These 121 conduct principles cover not only what we should do but also what we should not do — especially aiming at the faults people make often and easily.

You probably have been familiar with some of the 121 principles, but not all. Even if you are familiar with all (or most), you probably may still violate some on occasion.

If you have ever violated any conduct principles in the past, just let it pass away. From now on you may have new conduct.

These 121 items are principles, not strict rules. It is indeed not easy to 100% abide by all of them all one's life. If you occasionally, having no other choices under some circumstances, slightly violate a principle without resulting in a remediless consequence, do not feel guilty too much. Refer to the relevant principles and their explanations or discussions in this book, examine the fault you made, and avoid doing it again.

This book is for your reference. It is unnecessary for you to agree on all contents. If you disagree on one portion of the contents, you probably can find many other ones nevertheless very useful to yourself. You may deduce other conduct rules from these principles, explanations and discussions, and particularly apply them to the special cases you encounter.

The partial overlaps among principles are unavoidable. The main reason is that the conduct principles are *inherently* partially overlapped. For the sake of the character of a handbook, in this book two principles may be separated and placed into two different items even if they have a partial overlap; often a reader of this handbook may wish to read at a time only the principle closest to what he or she needs then.

On the other hand, the partial overlaps among principles also have the following consequence. If you think there are any conduct principles not covered by this book, then they probably can be deduced from or implied by some of the 121 principles. Hence, although this book has only 121 principles, it should be complete for good conduct in the *21st* century; if you are able to well deduce other conduct rules from these 121 principles and also well apply them, the 121 principles should be sufficient for all you need for good conduct in the *21st* century.

In the explanations or discussions of many items I suggest referring to some other relevant ones. Such cross-references can make effects better. However the suggestion signs for the cross-references are necessarily incomplete; particularly because what a reader needs varies with person and case and, as stated above, conduct principles are inherently partially overlapped. I thus do not try to make such signs complete. If you wish to see all of what you need, it should be better to look for them with the methods suggested in the *How to Use This Handbook*.

In order to be concise, a principle title may be an adjective (omitting "Be") unless a principle title of verb or noun is placed in the same item.

As for other helpful explanations and discussions, please see the *Preface*.

1. Honest

Don't cheat. Don't lie. Every word you say is true as you know.

In case one cannot tell the truth in one's mind, one would rather not say. When you have to say, what you say should be true as you know.

Have other people believe that every word you say is true. Build this credit, and don't let it be damaged.

Also see # 2, 28, 35, 36, 37, 61, 82.

2.

Sincere;

Cordial

Treating people, we should be sincere, cordial, honest, and true-hearted.

Also see # 1, 28, 75, 101, 103.

3.

Keep Faith;
Keep Your Promises;
Keep Your Words;
Be Careful in Making a Promise;
Lay Emphasis
on Faith and on Promise

You should fulfill your promises and words.

Don't carelessly make a promise or an engagement you later on cannot keep. If you cannot keep a promise, don't make it. If you are not sure that you can carry out a thing, don't promise. Once you make a promise, you should fulfill it.

Should you really be unable to keep a promise or an engagement, you should notify the person with whom you made it as soon as possible and should make an apology for that.

Also see # 38, 82, 99.

4. Humble

Don't be arrogant.

Humbleness may prevent one from being overly self-complacent, so that he or she may make more progress.

You may have proper pride in your mind, but this does not mean you may show insolence.

In the *21st* century competitions will be getting ever stronger, so it will be more likely that arrogance, boast, exaggeration and insolence provoke jealousy and/or dislike; on the contrary, humbleness may make you more respected by others.

When you need to describe something related to yourself, don't let the description exceed the fact.

Also see # 46, 69, 70.

5. Respect Other People

Respecting other people is a basic mind and attitude for good conduct.

One should not have sayings or doings of sneer. Even if any people have defects in ability, body, appearance, etc., don't sneer at them; we nevertheless should respect them.

As for people of low ranks, younger people, and younger generations, or when we help others or tip others, ..., we should still respect and be courteous to them.

Respect other person, and then he or she will respect you more.

Also see # 27, 104–112, 115.

6.

Upright;
Righteous

Always insist on uprightness and righteousness in your mind.

Don't oppress the good and fear the evil; don't bully the weak and dread the strong.

Don't take advantage of others' weakness or unsophisticatedness. If one is kindhearted or pure, he/she should not be used or oppressed.

Good people and good deeds should be rewarded.

Also see # 34, 35.

7. Tolerant

In this world it is impossible that everything goes perfectly as you wish. In this world any two persons are not completely the same, so other person's opinions may often different from yours. Associating with other people, one should be tolerant as much as possible.

Also see # 58, 73.

8. Help Other People

Within your capacity, help other people as you can.

Help not only acquaintances but also strangers when needed.

Helping other person may give yourself pleasure.

Besides traditional visible helps involving materials or tasks, in the *21st* century invisible helps will be growing ever more important — such as offering knowledge or advice, giving comforts or encouragements, and other spiritual supports. These may also benefit others' health (see the latter part of the *Preface* for details).

Also see # 11, 49, 50.

9. Respect Other Person's Privacy

Don't pry into other person's privacy. Avoid asking questions involving other person's privacy.

Often one's intention is only to concern oneself with other person or to have another positive mind, but he/she unconsciously violates this principle. Hence, be extra careful about this principle.

The respect for privacy and "personal space" will be growing ever more important in the *21st* century. To adapt oneself to the new society, one should be aware of this principle and follow it carefully.

Also see # 10.

10. Keep an Appropriate Distance

In the Eastern culture there is a saying: "The friendship between two superior persons is as insipid as water." It will be getting ever more suitable in the *21st* century.

In English it is customary to use "*close*" (or not) to describe the degree of a friendship. This reflects many people's minds. In fact, a more appropriate adjective for measuring the degree of a friendship should be "*good*" — how good, rather than "*close*" — how close. A good friend is not necessarily close; a close friend is not necessarily good.

Numerous people have a misconception that being close can certainly improve a friendship. But actually being too close may often spoil a friendship.

Respect a friend's privacy and "personal space"

(see # 9 for details).

Keeping an appropriate distance can help maintain a friendship — not only help maintain its degree, but also help make it more lasting (also see # 103).

11.

Sympathy;
Compassion

Always bear sympathy and compassion in your heart, for other people's pitiful misfortunes, for all people, and for all natural objects.

Also see # 49, 50.

12. Humor

Humor is a lubricant for association among people. It may also bring one oneself and others pleasure, and may add fun into lives. Therefore, be humorous under appropriate circumstances. Also, often have a sense of humor in your mind.

Showing humor should be adequate, and should be performed at appropriate times and places. Otherwise it may result in some negative effects.

It is habitual for many people to show humor by sneering, jeering and/or teasing others. Don't do it this way.

Numerous people are apt to show they are very humorous by saying sexual jokes. This kind of jokes is indeed likely to make an audience burst into laughter, but is suitable only for spouses and the like. One can be a really excellent humorist only if he/she is able to well show humor without sexual jokes, teases, etc.

Also see # 76, 115.

13. Good Manners

Have good manners like a real gentleman/lady.

Also see # 14, 29, 30, 32, 33, 44, 51, 76, 77, 79, 112, 115.

14.

Fine Chih-Jyr;

that is,
Fine Outward Manifestation of
Temperament and Disposition

Be careful about your own *Chih-Jyr*, and well cultivate it. This will get others to like you more, and will increase your own senses of honor, self-respect and self-confidence.

Also see # 13, 19, 29, 36, 51, 76, 77, 79. 115.

15.

Appreciating and Rewarding Your Parents;

Filial Piety

Filial piety is a traditional virtue in the Eastern culture.

Our parents have given so great much for raising and educating us; shouldn't we fulfill filial piety?

Appreciate and reward your parents. Within your capacity and the reasonable extent, do your best to give your parents what they wish.

16. Incorruptness

Don't be corrupt. Don't offer or accept a bribe. Don't be greedy for unreasonable money or goods.

Distinguish between the public and the private properties. Don't take or use the money or stuffs you should not.

Also see # 6, 35, 37, 74, 116.

17.

Fair;

Just

Have you ever thought of the feelings of the people unfairly treated? Haven't you ever sympathized with them? Haven't you yourself ever been unfairly treated? Guess other person's feelings by your own. Always treat people as fairly and justly as you can.

Also see # 6, 11, 25, 34, 35, 64, 104–111.

18. Understand Yourself

Understand yourself in various aspects, especially including your points of excellence and defect; overcome the latter and enhance the former.

Examine yourself from time to time, try to understand your own disposition, temperament, personality, emotion, sensation, motivation, desire, sentiment, etc., try to make a systematic analysis, enhance your points of superiority, and correct those of inferiority.

These may benefit your conduct. Also see # 19, 71, 72.

19.

Self-respect;
Self-confidence;
Elimination of the
Sense of Inferiority

Understand your own points of excellence, enhance them as you can, and cultivate your senses of self-respect and self-confidence. Don't have the *sense of inferiority* (inferiority complex), a big source of bad conduct, which may cause a series of defects in conduct and even some big mistakes.

If you have the *sense of inferiority*, try to eliminate it. Think of your points of excellence so as to cultivate your senses of self-respect and self-confidence. Follow the conduct principles in this book, so that you will at least win other people's respects and trusts. These will significantly help reduce your *sense of inferiority*. After it is eliminated, you may no longer be emotionally greatly upset for other person's tease, sneer, jeer, disdain, incorrect criticism, or trifles.

Also see # 18, 82, 85.

20.

Try to Understand Other Person; Avoid Misunderstanding

The following two points may be helpful for your conduct: (1) Understand the fundamental human nature. (2) Try to understand the person you treat, especially including understanding his or her motivation, thinking, sentiments and feelings.

Many relationships need to be judged with your own wisdom. They can not be completely understood merely in terms of spoken words, particularly since in general only a small portion of one's inner world is expressed in the way of spoken words.

Not understanding or even misunderstanding other person is often the source of many problems.

Also see # 21, 23, 24.

21.

Don't
Overestimate or Underestimate
a Friendship Too Much

If you overestimate a friendship too much, you will be disappointed. This may result in some bad psychological reactions.

If you underestimate a friendship too much, you may appear cold. He or she may bear a grudge against you, and that may cause many mistakes.

If the understanding and the expectation about a friendship are not far from the reality, those may be helpful for the stability and lasting of the friendship.

Also see # 20, 22, 23, 24, 103.

22.

When You Use
a Modern Communication Tool,
Unless Necessary,
Don't Expect
an Excessively Quick Response
from a Friend

In long times past mankind's main communication tool is letter mail. During the 20th century the telephone was invented earlier and FAX & various computer communication ways were invented more recently, so that messages can arrive immediately. In the *21st* century there will be more modes of communication, and they will be faster than ever.

In the past time of letter mail, the sender generally did not anticipate an immediate response. The recipient thus could arrange his or her tasks in order and respond in a reasonable time, and this did not make the sender unhappy.

Using modern communication tools which can have messages arrive immediately, such as e-mails, many senders are apt to expect to receive quick responses. If a recipient does not put his/her own tasks aside and respond at once, then this may get the sender to be disappointed, to have the feeling of frustration, or even to cherish grievances.

It is easy for modern communication to simultaneously send a message to lots of people. Many announcements, advertisements, ..., etc. take advantage of such a convenience. As a consequence, many people often receive a large number of "garbage messages", interfering with urgent work. While one is tired from dealing with a great number of "garbage messages", he or she may neglect an important message and delay the response.

The purpose of developing modern communication tools is for people's convenience and welfare. But in some cases those tools unexpectedly cause people trouble and even hurt friendships, especially for those people who do not realize this point and/or do not know how to well handle this matter.

Sending a message to a friend with a modern communication tool, such as an e-mail, you should realize this point. Unless necessary, don't expect an excessively quick response from a friend. Don't put pressure on your friend. You may even tell the friend that he/she may respond at his/her convenience. This shows your consideration and tolerance.

Communicating with a friend should not unexpectedly hurt the friendship, and should improve or maintain it as you expect.

In some cases, for improving or maintaining friendships, traditional letters and cards still have some func-

tions and merits hard to be replaced.

Also see # 20, 23, 24.

23.

Your Expectation Should Not Exceed the Reality Too Much

In addition to the principles # 21, 22 above, in general, one will probably be disappointed if one's expectation exceeds the reality too much. Furthermore, this may cause some bad psychological reactions, which may even be harmful for his/her conduct. Therefore that should be avoided.

Also see # 20, 21, 22.

24.

Be Considerate to Others;

Think from
Other Person's Point of View

Don't think always only at your own point of view;
do often from other person's. Be considerate to other
people.

Also see # 20, 22, 25, 26, 27.

25.

Guess Other Person's Feelings by Your Own;

Place Yourself in Another's Place

In the Eastern culture there is a saying: "Don't do to others that which you do not wish to be done to yourself."

Guess other people's feelings according to your own. But be cautious — other person's feeling may be different from your own.

Also see # 20, 24.

26.

Don't Build Your Joy
upon Other Person's Pain

Let yourself be happy, but don't make other person consequently painful.

Don't scold or exude your anger to an innocent for getting yourself to be pleasant.

Also see # 24, 25.

27.

Enjoy Freedom
but Don't Disturb Other People

Enjoy your own freedom but limit yourself. These self-constraints often have no definite boundaries. A good principle for this is: Don't disturb other person. For example, enjoy listening songs but don't disturb other people.

Also see # 24, 25, 26, 113.

28.

Being Houh-Dau;

that is,
Blend of Being Kindhearted, Being Generous, Being Honest and Being Considerate

This is a traditional virtue in the Eastern culture.

Don't be mean, stingy, deceitful or thoughtless to other people, and, instead, one should be *houh-dau* to others.

Also see # 1, 2, 6, 24, 31, 49.

29.

Propriety;
Courtesy

Do whatever we should regarding propriety and courtesy; don't be stingy with that.

Also see # 13, 14.

30. Kind

Be kind, nice, amiable, and cordial to other people.

Also see # 5, 32, 49.

31. Generous

Within your own capacity, be generous to other people; don't be stingy, miserly to others.

32. Harmonious

Associate with people harmoniously. Avoid hate, enmity or hostility as possible.

Also see # 30, 33.

33.

Do As Other People Like
under Some Circumstances

On friendly or social occasions, under the condition that other conduct principles are not violated, try to do as other people like as you can.

Also see # 30, 32.

34.

Distinguish Clearly
between Right and Wrong &
between Good and Evil

In your mind always distinguish clearly between right and wrong & between good and evil. You should direct your sayings and doings toward right and good & away from wrong or evil.

Also see # 6, 35, 37.

35. Moral Sense

Bear the *Moral Sense* permanently in your mind, and your sayings and doings should follow it. Even if other people's *Moral Senses* wither, you should still insist on it; don't allow it to weaken.

Also see # 6, 34, 83.

36. Sense of Honor

If one seeks only for material enjoyment all one's life, won't it be pitiable as to one of the human beings very superior to all the other animals? Some conduct principles in this book may greatly enhance the meaning of human life, and the *Sense of Honor* is one of them.

One should know whether a thing is honorable or not, and let it be one of references for choosing one's sayings and doings.

Also see # 37.

37. Sense of Shame

For the same reason as # 36, "*Sense of Honor*", one should know whether a thing is shameful or not and let it be one of references for choosing one's sayings and doings.

Also see # 36.

38. Sense of Responsibility

Bear the *Sense of Responsibility* permanently in your mind. Consider the consequence first, and then make a responsible decision. Take the responsibility for what you have said and for what you have acted. Take the responsibility for what you have done to people and to things. Don't shift your responsibility on to anyone else.

To ourselves, families, relatives, friends, groups to which we belong, society, mankind, the world, and all natural objects, we should have the *Sense of Responsibility*.

39.

Yih-Chi;

that is,
Blend of Faith, Righteousness,
Being Careful of Friendships,
Being Faithful to Friends, and
Appreciation & Reward for Favors

This is a traditional excellent spirit in the Eastern culture.

Be careful of friendships. Within your capacity, make appropriate expressions to friends on appropriate occasions.

Receiving a favor from someone, you should bear gratitude in your heart. Within your capacity, give appropriate rewards on appropriate occasions.

Even though long time has passed since then, that gratitude should still exist in your mind.

Also see # 103.

40. Don't Be Meddlesome

Most adults have their own opinions in minds, and have, more or less, some self-respects and self-confidences. If one is meddlesome and apt to force his/her opinions on others, then he/she may offend others easily.

Except for subordinates, younger generations, juniors, youths, *et al.*, unless necessary, you should offer your opinion *after* one sincerely asks it or you are sure that one sincerely wishes to listen it.

The opinion you offer to other person is a suggestion; don't force him/her to accept it. Allow him/her to make the final decision. After offering it, you have done your part; unless necessary, don't pursue to push him/her to follow it.

41.

Don't Transfer Anger from One Matter/Person to Another

Many people take it for granted that they may transfer their anger from one matter/person to another, and some think with confidence it is justifiable or even right and explain: "I was in the bad mood!" A lot of people make apologies for transferring anger: "I am sorry! I was then in the very bad mood." If one transfers anger only a few times, thereafter knows that behavior is a fault, and never does it again, then this is forgivable. If one endlessly continues to transfer anger because he/she does not realize that behavior is a fault or because he/she does not correct it even after he/she knows it is a fault, then this is a big mistake.

If you get angry about a matter, confine your anger only to that matter; if you get angry with a person, confine your anger only to that person. Understand and talk reason. Don't transfer your anger from one matter/person to another.

Under any circumstances and no matter how bad a mood you are in, you should never exude your own unpleasantness or anger to different matters or to innocents, including people living or working with you.

Also see # 34, 42, 43, 53, 54, 56, 57.

42.

Don't Act Only According to Your Emotions without Restraint

For treating people, don't act only according to your emotions. It should be rational, reasonable and self-restrained, and should follow the conduct principles in this book.

Also see # 24, 26, 27, 34, 35, 41, 43, 53, 55, 56, 57.

43.

Don't Cause People Around Pains or Unpleasantnesses

No matter how bad a mood you are in, you yourself should be responsible for trying to solve the problem and, as you can, avoid causing people around pains or unpleasantnesses.

Note that this item is not the same as # 41, *"Don't Transfer Anger from One Matter/Person to Another"*. *"Transferring Anger"* means exuding one's anger resulting from an unrelated matter to innocents. The *"Causing People Around Pains or Unpleasantnesses"* in this item not necessarily refers to anger. Many sayings or doings may make people around painful or unpleasant.

Also see # 24, 25, 26, 27, 34, 35, 38, 41, 42, 53, 55, 56.

44. Ethics of Competitions

In the *21st* century competitions will be getting ever stronger, so this conduct principle will be growing ever more important.

Don't pull the competitor's leg backward. You should truly win a competition, relying upon your own righteous efforts and strength.

You need not have the competitor fail or slow, and both may progress. Such a competition can prompt you to make more efforts so as to make even better progress.

Also see # 45, 46, 47, 48, 58.

45.

Avoid Being Jealous
of Other Person

In the Eastern culture there is a saying: "No matter how high a heaven is, there is another heaven higher than it; no matter how great a man is, there is another greater than him." In the human world, there is no way against the fact. Thus one may consider it to be natural.

If one's achievement is better than you, don't being jealous of him/her. Do your best to strive to accomplish your object. No matter how much you achieve, the best thing is that you have done your best; feel no regret for it, and have peace of mind.

Also see # 44, 46, 48, 58.

46.

Avoid That
Other Person Is Jealous of You

Although completely avoiding it is difficult, you should avoid as you can that other person is jealous of you.

Particularly as in the *21st* century competitions will be getting ever stronger, one should give even more care to doing it.

Being humble and respecting other people may greatly help you do it.

Understanding the fundamental human nature, trying to understand other person, thinking from other person's point of view, being considerate to others, *et al.* may tremendously help you do it, too.

Also see # 4, 5, 20, 24, 44, 45, 69, 70.

47.

Don't Rely
on the Competitor's Fall
but on Your Own Rise
for a Competition

For a competition don't rely on the competitor's failure or fall, but wholly on your own righteous efforts & strength and striving to make progress. This lets you concentrate your attention upon your own efforts, so that you may make even better progress. Winning in a competition this way is more honorable and admirable.

Also see # 36, 44.

48. Never Do Harm to Other Person

Whether for a competition or for other things, never do harm to other person.

Also see # 44, 45.

49.

Love;

Benevolence;

Mercy;

Charity;

Humanity;

Virtue

Always treat all people with love, benevolence, mercy, charity, humanity and virtue.

Also see # 11, 28, 35, 50.

50. Broad Love

Broaden your mind, and love not only all people but also all natural objects.

Bearing such a broad-love mind may make your whole mind broader, and then this will make you more magnanimous and you will bother less about the trifles of some unworthy affairs of relations among people.

Also see # 11, 49, 58, 73, 85.

51. Steady

Don't be flighty. Don't be too clamorous or loquacious. Don't be reckless or rash.

Also see # 13, 14, 52, 53, 54, 76, 77, 115.

52. Careful in Speaking

It is said that "calamities come from the mouth". Be careful in speaking. One should think first: will saying so result in any bad consequence? does saying so violate any conduct principle? At the beginning of this way you may feel the process is slow. After this habit is developed, the thinking will be faster. (This may promote your ability of faster thinking.)

Also see # 51, 61, 69, 76, 80, 81, 90, 114, 115.

53.

Never Be Impulsive;
Never Lose Self-Control

Under any circumstances, never be impulsive and never lose self-control. Numerous people rush into great calamities just on the impulse of the moment. Impulse often results in a remediless distressful consequence; they usually feel regret later, but it is too late.

Many people have a misconception that exuding anger to other person is a good way to eliminate the anger. In fact, that way often augments and/or extends the anger, makes the problem bigger, and even gets a regretful result.

When you are about to be impulsive, take a deep breath and think of the relevant conduct principles in this book so as to control yourself and to adjust your emotion. Think the problem from a different point of view; for example, do it from a more optimistic angle. See next several principles to get further help.

Also see # 7, 41, 51, 52, 54, 55, 56, 58.

54. Calm

When you encounter an unexpected and undesirable event or something which may make you angry or impulsive, calm yourself down. Being impulsive or rash usually makes things worse; calm may let oneself go in the right direction.

Also see # 51, 53, 55, 56.

55. Bearing

In this world it is impossible that everything goes perfectly as you wish. It is said that during one's life most events do not follow his/her wishes. When you encounter an undesirable matter involving person(s), you should bear the unpleasantness and then well handle it according to the conduct principles in this book.

Also see # 53, 54

56. Rational

Whether one deals with matter or people, one's thinkings, judgments and decisions should be based mainly upon rationality; one should not overly emotionalize one's deeds. Emotion should aid rationality, and should not conflict with it; rationality should well guide emotion, but should not eliminate it.

Also see # 41, 42, 57

57. Talk Reason

Treating people, speaking, conversation, negotiation and so on should talk reason. All your sayings and doings should be reasonable. You should have other people agree with you not only by mouth but also by mind.

Also see # 34, 42, 56, 69, 91.

58. Broad-minded

Cultivate your mind to make it broader. Treat people with respect, toleration and bearing as mush as possible.

Also see # 5, 7, 44, 45, 50, 55, 72, 73, 84, 85, 104–111, 117–120.

59. Don't Speak Ill of Others

Speaking ill of others is bad conudct; don't do it.

Also see # 7, 28, 48, 49, 52, 58, 60.

60. Avoid Criticizing a Third Person

Avoid criticizing a third person, unless necessary. There may be some exceptions; for example, the third person is a public figure, such as a politician, a figure reported in media.

If you are in the habit of criticizing a third person, then other person may suspect you also criticized him/her in front of a third party. This may damage his/her trust and respect for you.

Also see # 7, 28, 48, 49, 52, 58, 59, 82.

61. True

Base your sayings on facts. Don't invent false information.

It should not be done that one says what one guesses or what one is not sure as if it were a certain fact.

Saying what you are not sure, you should express the uncertainty. For examples, you may add "I guess", "possibly", "probably", "maybe", "perhaps", "should (be)", "seem", "appear", "I hope", "I wish", "I think", "I am not sure", ..., etc.

Also see # 69, 76, 80, 81, 82.

62. Optimistic

This principle refers to optimism in reasonable extent, not including unreasonable optimism.

Optimism makes one's daily life more active, makes one's whole life more meaningful, and makes one less depressed, dejected or despairing when he/she encounters challenge, difficulty, frustration or setback.

Your optimistic mind and attitude may bring others comfort and/or pleasantness, and may also let others be more optimistic.

Recently science confirms optimism benefits health. Thus optimism may benefit both your own and others' health. (Please see the latter part of the *Preface* for details.)

63.

Courageous;
Firm, Unyielding and Strong

When one is supposed to be courageous, be so; don't be afraid or cowardly.

When one is supposed to be firm, unyielding and strong, be so; don't be weak or spineless.

Also see # 64, 85.

64.

Independence;

Unless Necessary, Don't Depend on Other People

Individual independence will be a trend of society in the *21st* century. A lot of work will be done by one oneself or by service agents. The society in the *21st* century will also facilitate work in this way more and more. In fact, well using a telephone *yellow pages* can do almost all things people used to consider the necessity of depending on relatives' and friends' helps. *Internet* can facilitate your work, too. Likewise, more and more things can be done or assisted with machines. Moreover, the rise of various service agencies can add much more conveniences. A person working for you is not necessarily an acquaintance. You earn money by doing other things, and you pay for the services of agencies working for you, giving you conveniences, etc. You get what you want, and they get what they want. Work is done pleasantly and straightforward without adding a burden in mind due to disturbance to acquaintances.

If one is still infatuated with the way in the old society, that is, if one still depends on relatives' and friends' helps, he/she will find it more and more difficult to adapt himself/herself to the new society. Particularly people will be busier in the *21st* century, so it will be more inappropriate to depend on relatives' and friends' helps.

In order to pleasantly adapt oneself to the society in the *21st* centurly, one should develop one's ability and habit of independence. First of all, change conceptionally:

Within one's capacity, help others as one can (also see # 8); on the other hand, one should be as independent as one can — unless there is an obstacle which can not be overcome, don't depend on the helps of relatives and friends; above all, don't have the mind of dependence.

Also see # 63, 87, 101.

The promotion and prevalence of this concept will benefit the manners and customs of the whole society. If everyone acquires a job, a position, a promotion, a prize, an award, money, ..., etc. not by means of relatives' and friends' helps, "connections", or other improper ways but by means of his/her own real endeavors and contributions, then the whole society will approach a fairer and juster state (also see # 17).

If this ideal state is attained or approached, then the belief that being a good person will lose nothing will be built in people's minds. This will prompt people to respect morality and goodness more, and then the whole society will be even better.

65. Open-minded

On social occasions, be appropriately open-minded; don't be too bigoted.

66. Straightforward

When one is supposed to be straightforward, be so — one's sayings and doings should be concise and forthright, not muddled.

67. Resolute

When one is supposed to be resolute, be so; don't be hesitant.

Make a careful consideration first; when one has to make a decision, don't hesitate.

68.

Action Is Better Than Speaking in Some Cases

Don't exaggerate or talk recklessly for tasks you have not yet done; it is often better that you say after you do. It is even worse that one only speaks recklessly and does not take action.

Also see # 69, 70.

69.

Don't Boast of Yourself;

Don't Brag of Yourself;

Don't Exaggerate;

Don't Talk Recklessly;

Don't Invent False Information

When you speak, be careful not to make these faults.

Your sayings should be based on facts; don't exaggerate. Don't be arrogant. Avoid show-off.

Also see # 4, 61, 68, 76, 81, 82.

70.

Unless Necessary,
Talk Less about Yourself
but Concern Yourself
More about Other People

Unless necessary, avoid talking mostly about yourself during a conversation; you should concern yourself more about the person with whom you are talking or about other people.

Also see # 68, 69, 94.

71. Self-examination

Examine from time to time your own thinkings, sayings and doings — are they right? or wrong? good? or bad?

When you encounter a trouble, don't only blame other person(s); you should examine yourself first.

You should also from time to time make the self-examination: whether you have violated any conduct principles in this book.

Also see # 18, 72.

72.

Have the Courage
to Acknowledge a Fault;

Correct It
When You Know a Fault

Finding you have made a fault, you should be courageous to acknowledge it, to apologize for it, and to correct it and should never make it again.

Also see # 18, 71.

73.

Magnanimous to Others;
Lenient to Others

You should be strict to conduct yourself, but should be magnanimous to others.

Forgive other person(s) as possible. Do your best to tolerate and pardon others.

Also see # 7, 50, 58.

74.

Don't Take Advantage of
Other Person's Weakness

Abide by uprightness and incorruptness. Don't take advantage of other person's weakness.

Also see # 6, 16.

75. Don't Use a Friend

Be careful of friendships, and treat your friends in righteous ways. Within your own capacity you should help your friends as much as you can, but you yourself should not use any real friend.

Also see # 2, 6, 8, 16, 64, 87, 101.

76.

Careful about
Your Style of Conversation

Be careful about your style of conversation; improve your manner of speaking and the words you use.

Many people have some defects in the style of conversation, neglected by themselves; such as using dirty, indecent or coarse words, excessively using *cliché*. One should be constantly careful about this, and should make efforts to correct it.

A lot of people habitually tease, sneer or jeer at others unconsciously during conversations, and/or show such manners or tones. This should be corrected. Use more respectful words, manners and tones.

Also see # 12, 13, 14, 29, 57, 61, 69, 80, 81, 82, 83, 88, 90, 114, 115.

77. Careful about Your Behavior

Many people have some defects in behavior. Such defects are countless. One may be aware of some of them oneself, but has already fallen into such bad habits and in consequence often and easily does them unconsciously. Therefore one should be constantly careful about his/her own behavior. If one finds any defect in it, make efforts to correct it and completely uproot the bad habit.

Also see # 13, 14, 78, 79, 115.

78.

Careful about Your Habits of Cleanliness and Hygiene

If one's habits of cleanliness and hygiene are bad, other people will dislike him/her and avoid his/her company.

Bad habits about hygiene may cause sickness either directly or via infection from another. Bad habits about cleanliness may often make one's body, clothes and articles dirty, may get other people to frown, and may cause sickness indirectly.

In the *21st* century people will be careful of health, cleanliness and hygiene more than ever, so this conduct principle will be growing ever more important.

Be careful about your cleanliness and hygiene, develop good habits, and always follow them.

Also see # 77.

79.

Develop Your Habits of Proper and Refined Behavior

One should constantly cultivate the habits of proper and refined behavior, and uproot any defect in it.

If one gets into any bad habits of defects in behavior, it is not easy to avoid all of them on social occasions. It is also not easy to have proper and refined behavior instantly; it is supposed to be constantly cultivated and developed for a long time into habits.

Also see # 13, 14, 77, 78, 115.

80.

Don't Make
an Arbitrary Implication

Arbitrary implication can be seen or heard almost everywhere and everyday. Most people do not clearly know it is incorrect. Many authors and speakers like to cite and praise quotations of arbitrary implication. Any reader of this section should from now on be aware of the unfortunate fact, and should not make arbitrary implication any more.

If A can not imply B, don't make such an implication. For example, "a part" can not imply "the whole", "usually" can not imply "always", etc. Numerous people often make such a mistake unawares.

For an uncertain thing, don't express the certainty. If a statement is based on any conditions or assumptions, indicate the latter when you state the former. If a statement is not "absolutely", "always", or "all", don't say so.

Don't "make the boat capsized and all the passengers fallen into the water if you intend to beat only one of them with a long rod".

To avoid making arbitrary implications, in your sayings you may add, for examples, "almost (all)", "most", "many", "a lot of", "some", "usually", "often", "sometimes", "under some conditions", "if ..., (then)...", ..., etc. In addition, those mentioned in # 61 may also help avoid such a mistake.

Also see # 61, 76, 81, 82.

81. Objective

When you think or speak, be objective as far as you can and avoid being subjective; often stand at others' points of view and avoid doing only at your own. Avoid prejudiced words.

If your words are subjective, indicate so, such as "I think", "in my opinion", etc.

Also see # 76, 80, 82.

82.

Creditable;
Trustworthy

Make your sayings believed and your doings trusted by other people. Carefully maintain this credit, and don't let it be damaged.

How do you build this credit? It can be achieved if you are able to follow the conduct principles in this book. For example, to make your words believed by others, you should be honest, sincere, cordial, careful in making a promise, fair, just, & objective and you should keep your promises & not make arbitrary implications and ...., etc. Likewise, you can maintain this credit if you continue to follow the conduct principles in this book without violation.

Also see # 1, 2, 3, 17, 61, 69, 80, 81.

83.

Showing Morality Is More Important Than Showing Cleverness

Numerous people subconsciously like to show cleverness, regardless of morality. To conduct oneself well, one should be aware that showing morality is more important than showing cleverness; the latter should be performed under the condition that morality and other conduct principles are not violated.

Also see # 34, 35.

84.

Don't Make
Mischiefs and Troubles
among People

Broaden your mind, and don't make mischiefs and troubles among people.

Also see # 58, 73, 85.

85.

Don't Bother about the Trifles of the Unworthy Affairs of Relations among People;

Don't Bother about Other Person's Incorrect Criticism

For those trifles of the unworthy affairs of relations among people, don't bother about them! Remember to broaden your mind and tolerate other people.

After you examine yourself and know you did not violate any conduct principle, then don't bother about other person's incorrect criticism! Remember to understand yourself, cultivate your senses of self-respect and self-confidence, eliminate the *sense of inferiority*, be optimistic and active, be courageous, firm, unyielding and strong, and have peace of mind.

Also see # 7, 18, 19, 50, 58, 62, 63, 71, 72, 73, 84.

86. Avoid Generating Enemies

Unless there is no better choice, avoid generating enemies as you can.

Also see # 49, 50.

87.

You Would Rather Be Owed by Other Person Than Owe Him/Her

Within your capacity, help others and make contributions as you can. Avoid owing other person.

Also see # 8, 28, 39, 101.

88.

Try to Interest Yourself in Another's Talk during a Friendly or Social Conversation

This is one of the bases for the success in social conversations, and also expresses your respect and friendliness to him/her.

Also see # 5, 33, 50, 89, 92.

89.

During a Social Conversation with Several Persons, Try to Take Care of All

This may avoid someone feels that you are arrogant, you think little of him/her, or even you dislike him/her. Moreover this is a right manner you should have.

Also see # 5, 13, 30, 33, 50, 88, 92.

90.

Don't
Curse or Grumble Arbitrarily

When a thing goes undesirably, one should calmly and rationally look for a way to handle it. Arbitrary curse or grumble may get people to think little of him/her, for this shows he/she is not cultivated.

Also see # 7, 41, 42, 43, 51, 52, 53, 54, 55, 56, 58.

91.

Consultation and Mutual Consent

It is inevitable that conflicts or disagreements, big or small, among people may happen. At this moment we should calmly and rationally consult with each other, and try to look for a solution of mutual consent.

Also see # 20, 24, 54, 56, 57, 118.

92. Friendly

Be friendly to others as you can. This also expresses your good manner, benevolence, broad love and respect to people.

Also see # 5, 13, 30, 32, 49, 50.

93. Warm

On appropriate occasions, be appropriately warm to other person(s). Don't be stingy with warmth. Don't be cold to others. Warmth can add pleasure into the human world.

Also see # 49, 92.

94.

Concern Yourself
about Other People

Under the condition that other conduct principles are not violated, you should appropriately concern yourself about other people, particularly including your family, relatives, friends and so on. Also,
within your capacity help them when needed; at least,
concern yourself about them in your heart.

Also see # 8, 9, 10, 11, 15, 30, 40, 49, 70.

95.

Don't Judge a Person by His/Her Outward Appearance

In the Eastern culture there is a saying: "As the total volume of sea water cannot be measured with a bushel, so one cannot be known by one's looks." Don't judge a person by his/her outward appearance.

Also see # 80, 96, 109.

96.

Don't Criticize or Tease Another's Outward Appearance

One's outward appearance cannot show whether one is good or bad, and its main factor is not determined by his/her will. Don't criticize or tease other person's outward appearance.

Also see # 5, 12, 49, 80, 95, 109.

97. Acknowledgment

Whether you accept another's help, advice, offer, hospitality and so on or not, you should express your thanks. Even if you do not accept it, don't say any bad words and don't be silent.

Also see # 13, 29.

98. Patient

Treating people, one should be patient.

99.

Keep Your Appointments on Time

Having an appointment with someone, you should keep it on time; avoid being late as you can.

Also see # 3, 38.

100.

Help Relieve Friends' Worries; Share Your Joy with Friends; Congratulate or Praise Friends

When a friend has a worry, under the condition that other conduct principles are not violated, within your own capacity you should try to help relieve it as you can.

Also see # 8.

If you have a joy, it is good to share your pleasure with friends.

When a friend shares his/her (righteous) joy with you, you should be happy for him/her.

When you are supposed to congratulate or praise a friend, do so; don't be stingy with congratulations or praise.

101.

Help Friends but Don't Intend to Gain Any Profit or Advantage from a Friend

It is not a righteous function of a real friendship to provide money, goods or other profits. A (real) friendship is different from a business relationship.

Within your capacity you should help friends as you can, but don't intend to gain any profit or advantage from a friend. This is a righteous attitude toward friendships.

Also see # 2, 8, 64, 74, 75, 87, 100.

102.

If You Want to Do a Thing, Do It Well

If we cannot do a thing well, we would rather not do it unless required.

If we are unable to do a thing well because there are too many things to do, then, if possible, we should choose to do those more worth doing; set priority and omit those more omissible in case of no time. Once we decide to do a thing, we should do it well.

This principle is suitable for social activities in the same way. If you are unable to follow any conduct principles because you have too many social activities, then you should make choices and omit some. We would rather lower the number of social activities so as to follow the conduct principles well.

103. Lasting

A real friendship should not fade as time passes, and should not weaken because of space separation.

Also see # 2, 39.

104.

Don't Discriminate against One According to One's Disability

Sympathize with one in one's disability, and help him/her as you can; don't discriminate against one according to one's disability.

Also see # 5, 8, 11.

105.

Don't Discriminate against One According to One's Race or Color

One's race was determined when one was born, and is not his/her own choice.

Any race has both kind and evil people. Don't make an arbitrary implication. Don't "make the boat capsized and all the passengers fallen into the water if you intend to beat only one of them with a long rod".

Broaden your mind, and respect other people. Don't discriminate against one according to one's race or color.

Also see # 5, 17, 58, 80, 81.

106.

Don't Discriminate against One According to One's Nationality or National Origin

The advance of science and technology, the improvement of traffic instruments and communication tools, the promotion of the knowledge and wisdom of mankind, and the rise of the sense of internationalization and the sense of the world make the "boundaries" between nations gradually faded. Sooner or later, hopefully in the *21st* century, the whole earth eventually will be united and will have real peace, and there will be no more fights among nations.

Nationality is nothing but a kind of paper work of artificial administrative categorization in this transition period. Its meaning will get lighter and lighter, and it will disappear eventually. In the mankind's long-term history, emphasizing or exaggerating nationality will be merely a small block of shortsighted hindrance on the road of the mankind's peace and unity evolution.

Any country has both kind and evil people. Don't make an arbitrary implication. Don't "make the boat capsized and all the passengers fallen into the water if you intend to beat only one of them with a long rod".

Broaden your mind, and respect other people. Don't discriminate against one according to one's nationality.

For the same reason, don't discriminate against one according to one's national origin.

Also see # 5, 17, 58, 80, 81, 107, 117, 118, 119, 120.

107.

Don't Discriminate against One According to One's State Residence, Region or Accent

In the old times the traffic was inconvenient, so the contacts among different regions were difficult. This resulted in a lot of languages and dialects. The difference of language or dialect made the communication of sentiments among people in different regions obstructed. Nowadays, particularly in the *21st* century, due to the improvement of traffic instruments and communication tools, the above "cause" approaches disappearance. However, the improvement regarding the above "result" is much slower than that regarding the above "cause". This is due to some weak points of the human nature, but also can be fixed by ourselves, the human beings.

Be farsighted, and think it wisely. This kind of discriminations due to different regions mainly originated from the traffic inconvenience in the old times. If one still sticks to such discriminations of old-time unwisdom in the *21st* century when the traffic and communication will be much better, then won't he/she be too shortsighted and narrow-minded?

The meaning of state residence is similar to that of region for this point, and merely has an extra factor of artificial administrative categorization.

One's native language is determined by the environment in which one began to learn to speak in one's babyhood, and is not his/her own choice. When two persons having different native languages talk with each other with the same language, it is mostly inevitable for them to have more or less different accents.

These all originated from the traffic inconvenience

in the old times. Such discriminations are unwise and irrational.

Understanding the background, in the *21st* century we should broaden our minds and respect other people even more and should not discriminate against one according to one's state residence, region or accent.

Also see # 5, 17, 56, 58, 80, 81, 106.

108.

Don't Discriminate against One According to One's Gender

Man and woman are equal. Broaden your mind and respect other person, whether the person is a man or a woman; don't discriminate against one according to one's gender.

Also see # 5, 17, 58.

109.

Don't Discriminate against One According to One's Outward Appearance

One's outward appearance cannot express whether one is kind or evil, and one's defects in outward appearance are mostly not due to his/her faults. Broaden your mind and respect other person, no matter what his/her outward appearance it is; don't discriminate against one according to one's outward appearance.

Also see # 5, 17, 58, 80, 95, 96.

110.

Don't Discriminate against One According to One's Poverty

There are many factors which may cause poverty. In most cases, one's poverty is not due to personal fault. In fact, from some points of view, poverty is often due to pitiful misfortune.

Broaden your mind and respect other people, and, within your capacity, sympathize with poor person(s) and help them; don't discriminate against one according to one's poverty.

Also see # 5, 8, 11, 80.

111.

Don't Discriminate against One According to One's Religion Choice

Religion choice is a personal freedom, and we should respect it. Broaden your mind and respect other people, and don't discriminate against one according to one's religion choice.

Also see # 5, 58, 81.

112. Democracy

One should have the cultivation and manner of democracy. Respect the opinions of the majority in group activities.

Also see # 13.

113. Sense of Public Morality

Don't only care for your own private advantages or conveniences. For all your deeds, big or small, be careful not to do harm to others or to the public.

Also see # 24, 26, 27.

114.

Don't Let
Your Sayings and Doings
Transgress What Is Proper

Under any circumstances, no matter what your emotion it is, don't let your sayings and doings transgress what is proper.

Also see # 12, 13, 51, 52, 53, 54, 56, 115.

115.

Be Careful!
Don't Make a Sexual Harassment

In the last decade of the 20th century the issue of sexual harassment shakes the whole US society. From the US President to all ranks in the US society, none of them can be immune from the suits or tangles about sexual harassments. The US society appears agitated and nervous on account of this; numerous people actively sue for having been sexually harassed, and numerous people are afraid of being sued for having made sexual harassments and/or for potentially doing them in the future. Upon being sued about a sexual harassment, usually one is down and often even out; at least one is disturbed and troubled very much.

Not all suits about sexual harassments are brought by women against men; many are done by men against women as well. Perhaps to many people's even greater surprise, the US law of sexual harassment may also be applied to the case that the accuser and the accused are the same gender.

In the *21st* century the problem of sexual harassment will continue to bluster in the US, and that hurricane will sweep other countries, too. A lot of nations and regions will adopt various laws of sexual harassment.

Many accuseds were unaware that it was a fault while making a sexual harassment, since in the past those sayings and doings had not been regarded as crimes and had not been universally considered faults and lots of people had already fallen into a habit of doing so. This is why I have added *"Be Careful!"* in the title of this principle to further remind readers. In the *21st* century people should be extra alerted not to make sexual harassments.

Many people may ask: "It seems very difficult to avoid making sexual harassments. How should I do it?" I think a useful and concise hint is: Let your speaking and behavior be like a gentleman/lady. It may appear trivial at your first glance, but actually not. Think over the hint so as to be able to well comprehend, digest and absorb it. If you used to consider it to be difficult to avoid making sexual harassments, you may try this way from now on.

In addition to that useful and concise hint in the preceding paragraph, a more thorough method of avoiding making sexual harassments is to follow the relevant conduct principles in this book. See, for examples, 5, 10, 12, 13, 14, 51, 52, 76, 77, 114.

116. Law-abiding

The law in the *21st* century will tend to be further detailed and complicated, and will make more limits and constraints to many kinds of personal freedom. The law of sexual harassment is an example (see # 115 for details). Many people's conceptions and habits will be different from what the law will ask, so it will become easier to violate the law if one is not careful. As a result, numerours people will break the law unawares in the *21st* century. Upon being accused of breaking the law, one will be disturbed and troubled a lot and/or even down and out, not to mention the possible loss of freedom.

To avoid breaking the law, one should pay attention to the relevant specific laws and solidify the law-abiding concept and habit.

For a constitutional, democratic, mature and healthy society in the *21st* century, it is desirable that everyone is law-abiding. If you consider a law to be bad, you may try to change it in some lawful ways. Before the change, we should still comply with it — at least do not break it.

Also see # 112.

117.

View of the International Society

As discussed in # 106, the human society in the *21st* century will approach much higher internationalization and multi-culture inter-blending. In the *21st* century the sense of internationalization will also rise greatly. We should even more be farsighted, broaden our minds, cultivate the view of the international society people should have in the *21st* century, and treat international societies and international people well.

Also see # 5, 58, 105, 106, 107, 111, 118, 119, 120.

118. View of Peace

People should live at peace with each other, and should not fight with each other.

Let's generalize this view of peace, so groups of people should live at peace with each other, and should not fight with each other. Likewise, different regions and societies should live at peace with each other, too.

As discussed in # 106 and 117, sooner or later, hopefully in the *21st* century, the whole earth eventually will be united and will have real peace and there will be no more fights among nations.

In the *21st* century, we should even more be far-sighted, broaden our minds, cultivate the view of peace people should have in the *21st* century, and treat all people with that view.

Also see # 5, 49, 50, 58, 91, 105, 106, 107, 111, 117, 119, 120.

119. View of the World

All human beings live on this very small earth, while the earth is only a tiny particle in the vast universe. Therefore all people all over the world are in the same boat, and should help instead of fighting with one another. People should have this understanding and mind.

As discussed in # 106, 117, 118, in the *21st* century the sense of the world will rise greatly, different cultures will inter-blend acceleratively, and, sooner or later, the whole earth eventually will be united and will have real peace.

In the *21st* century we should even more be far-sighted, broaden our minds, eliminate the old-time narrow-minded sense of regions, cultivate the view of the world people should have in the *21st* century, treat people all over the world with that view, and give more care and protection to our lovely little earth.

Also see # 5, 50, 58, 106, 107, 117, 118, 120.

120.

View of Dah-Turng
in the 21st Century;

that is, Blended View of
Universal Harmony,
a Nice Human Society, and
Sharing the World with All People

As discussed in # 104–111, 117, 118, 119, in the
21st century we, all human beings, should even more
be farsighted, broaden our minds, no longer stick to
the shortsighted narrow-minded sense of regions and
boundaries, no longer discriminate against one another, have the understanding and mind that we all
are in the same boat and should help instead of fighting with one another, live at peace with one another,
and protect and enjoy together our wonderful world.

Also see # 5, 50, 58, 104–111, 117, 118, 119.

121. Consistent

Your conduct should be consistent. Your thinkings, sayings and doings should be consistent.

Following the preceding conduct principles should be consistent. Always follow them rather than sometimes do while other times not. Treat all people with them rather than treat some with them while do others not.

Perhaps some people may ask: "Since the relationships among people are different — closer or more distant, why can we treat all people with the same principles?" The answer is: There is indeed a difference of degree for treating people because of the relationship difference — closer or more distant, but the conduct principles are the same.

Consistency may also make your conduct in the *21st* century simpler, easier and even better.

Principle Index

Principle Title • Item No.

A

Acknowledgment • 97

Action Is Better Than Speaking in Some Cases • 68

Appreciating and Rewarding Your Parents • 15

Avoid Being Jealous of Other Person • 45

Avoid Criticizing a Third Person • 60

Avoid Generating Enemies • 86

Avoid Misunderstanding • 20

Avoid That Other Person Is Jealous of You • 46

B

Be Careful! Don't Make a Sexual Harassment • 115

Be Careful in Making a Promise • 3

Be Considerate to Others • 24

Bearing • **55**

Being *Houh-Dau* • **28**

Benevolence • **49**

Blend of Being Kindhearted, Being Generous, Being
  Honest and Being Considerate • **28**

Blend of Faith, Righteousness, Being Careful of
  Friendships, Being Faithful to Friends, and
  Appreciation & Reward for Favors • **39**

Blended View of Universal Harmony, a Nice Human
  Society, and Sharing the World with All People
  • **120**

Broad Love • **50**

Broad-minded • **58**

C

Calm • **54**

Careful about Your Behavior • **77**

Careful about Your Habits of Cleanliness and Hygiene
  • **78**

Careful about Your Style of Conversation • **76**

Careful in Speaking • **52**

Charity • 49

Compassion • 11

Concern Yourself about Other People • 94

Congratulate or Praise Friends • 100

Consistent • 121

Consultation and Mutual Consent • 91

Cordial • 2

Correct It When You Know a Fault • 72

Courageous • 63

Courtesy • 29

Creditable • 82

D

Democracy • 112

Develop Your Habits of Proper and Refined Behavior
• 79

Distinguish Clearly between Right and Incorrect & between Good and Evil • 34

Do As Other People Like under Some Circumstances
• 33

Don't Act Only According to Your Emotions without

Restraint • **42**

Don't Be Meddlesome • **40**

Don't Boast of Yourself • **69**

Don't Bother about Other Person's Incorrect Criticism
• **85**

Don't Bother about the Trifles of the Unworthy Affairs
of Relations among People • **85**

Don't Brag of Yourself • **69**

Don't Build Your Joy upon Other Person's Pain • **26**

Don't Cause People Around Pains or Unpleasantnesses
• **43**

Don't Criticize or Tease Another's Outward Appearance • **96**

Don't Curse or Grumble Arbitrarily • **90**

Don't Depend on Other People • **64**

Don't Discriminate against One According to One's
Disability • **104**

Don't Discriminate against One According to One's
Gender • **108**

Don't Discriminate against One According to One's
Nationality or National Origin • **106**

Don't Discriminate against One According to One's Outward Appearance • **109**

Don't Discriminate against One According to One's Poverty • **110**

Don't Discriminate against One According to One's Race or Color • **105**

Don't Discriminate against One According to One's Religion Choice • **111**

Don't Discriminate against One According to One's State Residence, Region or Accent • **107**

Don't Exaggerate • **69**

Don't Invent False Information • **69**

Don't Judge a Person by His or Her Outward Appearance • **95**

Don't Let Your Sayings and Doings Transgress What Is Proper • **114**

Don't Make a Sexual Harassment • **115**

Don't Make an Arbitrary Implication • **80**

Don't Make Mischiefs and Troubles among People • **84**

Don't Overestimate or Underestimate a Friendship

Too Much • **21**

Don't Rely on the Competitor's Fall but on Your Own
Rise for a Competition • **47**

Don't Speak Ill of Others • **59**

Don't Talk Recklessly • **69**

Don't Take Advantage of Other Person's Weakness •
74

Don't Transfer Anger from One Matter/Person to Another • **41**

Don't Use a Friend • **75**

During a Social Conversation with Several Persons,
Try to Take Care of All • **89**

E

Elimination of the Sense of Inferiority • **19**

Enjoy Freedom but Don't Disturb Other People • **27**

Ethics of Competitions • **44**

F

Fair • **17**

Filial Piety • **15**

Fine *Chih-Jyr* • 14

Fine Outward Manifestation of Temperament and Dis-

position • 14

Firm, Unyielding and Strong • 63

Friendly • 92

G

Generous • 31

Good Manners • 13

Guess Other Person's Feelings by Your Own • 25

H

Harmonious • 32

Have the Courage to Acknowledge a Fault • 72

Help Friends but Don't Intend to Gain Any Profit or

Advantage from a Friend • 101

Help Other People • 8

Help Relieve Friends' Worries • 100

Honest • 1

Houh-Dau • 28

Humble • 4

Humanity • 49

Humor • 12

I

If You Want to Do a Thing, Do It Well • 102

Incorruptness • 16

Independence • 64

J

Just • 17

K

Keep an Appropriate Distance • 10

Keep Faith • 3

Keep Your Appointments on Time • 99

Keep Your Promises • 3

Keep Your Words • 3

Kind • 30

L

Lasting • 103

Law-abiding • 116

Lay Emphasis on Faith and on Promise • 3

Lenient to Others • 73

Love • 49

M

Magnanimous to Others • 73

Mercy • 49

Moral Sense • 35

N

Never Be Impulsive • 53

Never Do Harm to Other Person • 48

Never Lose Self-control • 53

O

Objective • 81

Open-minded • 65

Optimistic • 62

P

Patient • 98

Place Yourself in Another's Place • 25

Propriety • **29**

R

Rational • **56**

Resolute • **67**

Respect Other People • **5**

Respect Other Person's Privacy • **9**

Righteous • **6**

S

Self-confidence • **19**

Self-examination • **71**

Self-respect • **19**

Sense of Honor • **36**

Sense of Public Morality • **113**

Sense of Responsibility • **38**

Sense of Shame • **37**

Share Your Joy with Friends • **100**

Showing Morality Is More Important Than Showing
Cleverness • **83**

Sincere • **2**

Steady • 51

Straightforward • 66

Sympathy • 11

T

Talk Less about Yourself but Concern Yourself More
about Other People • 70

Talk Reason • 57

Think from Other Person's Point of View • 24

Tolerant • 7

True • 61

Trustworthy • 82

Try to Interest Yourself in Another's Talk during a
Friendly or Social Conversation • 88

Try to Understand Other Person • 20

U

Understand Yourself • 18

Unless Necessary, Don't Depend on Other People • 64

Unless Necessary, Talk Less about Yourself but Concern Yourself More about Other People • 70

Upright • **6**

V

View of *Dah-Turng* in the *21st* Century • **120**

View of the International Society • **117**

View of Peace • **118**

View of the World • **119**

Virtue • **49**

W

Warm • **93**

When You Use a Modern Communication Tool, Unless
Necessary, Don't Expect an Excessively Quick
Response from a Friend • **22**

Y

Yih-Chi • **39**

You Would Rather Be Owed by Other Person Than
Owe Him/Her • **87**

Your Expectation Should Not Exceed the Reality Too
Much • **23**

General Index

A

ability 40,103
accent 142-144
acknowledge 110
acknowledgment 133
active 100,123
adjective 13,45
adult 8,79
advantage 41,60,112,136,149
advice 43,133
afraid 101
age 11
agriculture era 2
Americans 5
amiable 69
anger 80-81,83,91
angry 80,93
animal 14,74
apologize 110
apology 38,80
appearance 40
appointment 134
appreciate 51,77
arbitrary implication 117,120,
         139,141
arrogance 39
arrogant 39,107,126
attitude 40,100,136

B

bad conduct 6,55
"Be" 13
bear 94
bearing 94,97
behavior 14-15,80,114,116,153
   kinder 15
   nicer 15
   proper 116
   refined 116
benefit, 13-16,43,54,100,104
   good conduct 13-16
benevolence 88,129
bigoted 105
board love 89,129
boast 39,107
body 40
bother 89,123
boundary 2,67,140,160
brag 107
brain 14
break the law 154-155
bribe 52
broaden one's mind 89,97,122,
         123,139,141,144-148,
         156-160
broad-minded 97
bushel 131
business relationship 136

C

calm 93,127,128
car 1
card 62
career 13
century,
  the 20th, 1,2,4,12,59,151
    last decade 151
    latter half 4
  the 21st, 1-8,11,13,15,16,39,
    43,44,45,59,86,102-104,
    115,140,142-144,152,154-
    155,156-161
  eve 8
challenge 4,100
charity 88
cheat 35
chih-jyr 50
clamorous 89
cleanliness 115
cleverness 121
cliché 113
Clinton, Bill, US President 5-6
close 45
coarse words 113
cold 58,129
color 139
comfort 2,43,100
communication tools 1,3,59-62
company 115
compassion 47
competition 39,84,86,87,88
complication 4
computer 59
computer communication ways
    59
concern 108,130
conduct,
  bad 6,55,97
  good 4,5,6,11,13-16,40
  new 9
  personal 6
conduct and health, 14-15
  relation 14-15
conduct education 5
conduct mind 8
conduct problem 6,7
  interest 7
conduct soul 8
conduct spirit 8
congratulate 135
congratulations 135
considerate 64,68,86
consideration 61,106
consistency 161
consistent 161
consult 128
consultation 128
contradiction 4
control, 5
  gun 5
conversation 96,108,113,125,126
cordial 35,69,120
correct 110,113,114
corrupt 52
country 3,5,141,152
courage 110
courageous 101,110,123
courteous 40
courtesy 69
cowardly 101
credit 35,120
creditable 120
crime 4,152
crisis, 5
  national 5
criticizing a third person 98
cross-reference 11

culture, 3,8,158
   Eastern 8,45,51,65,68,77,85, 131
   Western 8
curse 127
customary factors 12
customs 3,104

D

dau-turng, 160
   in the 21st century 160
deceitful 68
defect 40,54,55,113,114,116,146
degree, 45-46,161
   friendship 45-46
dejected 100
democracy 149
depressed 100
despairing 100
desire 54
destiny, 4
   mankind's 4
dialect 142-144
dirty words 113
disability 138
disappointed 58,60,63
disaster 4
discriminate 138-148,160
discrimination, 138-148
   accent 142-144
   color 139
   disability 138
   gender 145
   national origin 140-141
   nationality 140-141
   outward appearance 146
   poverty 147
   race 139
region 142-144
religion choice 148
state residence 142-144
disdain 56
dislike 39,115,126
disposition 50,54
distance 1,2,45-46
disturb 67,151,154
disturbance 103
drug abuses 4

E

earth 140,157,158-159
   our lovely little 159
Eastern culture 8,45,51,65,68,77, 85,131
economic factors 2
educate 51
education, 5
   conduct 5
e-mail 1,60-61
emotion 14-15,54,82,92,95,150
   pleasanter 15
   stabler 15
emotionalize 95
encouragement 2,43
enemy 124
engagement 35
English 45
enmity 70
equal 145
ethics 1,84
   competition 84
exaggerate 106,107,141
exaggeration 39
expectation 58,63
exude one's anger 66,81,83,91

F

fair 53,104,120
faith 37,77
faithful 77
family, 13,76,130
    big 2
    small 2
farsighted 143,156-160
fault 9,80,107,110,146,147,152
favor 77
FAX 1,59
filial piety 51
finances 2
firm 101,123
fights 140,157,158,160
flighty 89
force 79
forgive 111
freedom, 27,148,154
    personal 2,3,148,154
friend 13,59-62,76,77,102-104,
        112,130,135,136
firendliness 125
friendly 129
friendship 2,45-46,58,61-62,77,
        112,136
    real 136,138
frustration 60,100
fundamental human nature 57,86

G

"garbage messages" 60
gender 12,13,145,152
generating enemies 124
generous 68,70
good conduct 4,5,6,11,13-16,40
goodness 104
government 5

grand kin complex 2
gratitude 77-78
greedy 52
grumble 127
gun control 5

H

habit 90,98,103,114,115,116,152,
        154
happiness, 4,13-14,15
    mankind's 4
harm 88,149
harmonious 70
hate 70
healing function 14
health, 6,14-15,43,100,115
    society 6
heart 47,77,130
help 40,43,56,86,102-104,112,
        124,130,133,135,136,
        138,147,158,160
    invisible 43
    visible 43
hesitant 106
hesitate 106
honest 35,36,68,120
honor 50,74
hospitality 133
hostility 70
houh-dau 68
How to Use This Handbook 11,
        27-28
human being 14,74,142,158,160
human society 4,16,156,160
humanities 1
humanity 88
humble 39,86
humbleness 39

humor 48-49
humorist 49
humorous 48
hygiene 115

I

immune system 14
implication,
    arbitrary 117,120,139,141
impulse 91
impulsive 91,93
incorrect criticism 56,123
incorruptness 52,112
indecent words 113
independence 2,102-104
individual system 2
inferiority complex 55,123
ingredients of conduct 14
inner world 57
insolence 39
inter-blending, 4,156,158
    multi-culture 4,156,158
international people 156
international society 156
internationalization 3,140,156
Internet 1,102
invent false information 107

J

jealous 85,86
jealousy 39
jeer 48,56,113
job 13,104
joke, 48
    sexual 48-49
joy 66,135
just 53,104,120

K

kind 69,139,141,146
kindhearted 41,68
knowledge 3,43,140

L

language 142-144
    native 143
lasting 46,58,138
law, 3,152,154-155
    sexual harassment 3,152,154
law-abiding 154-155
lenient 111
letter 59-62
lie 35
life 2
living 2
logic 1
looks 131
loss self-control 91
loquacious 89
love, 88,89
    board 89,129

M

magnanimous 89,111
make a promise 37
man 12,16,145,151
man and woman 12,145
managements 2
mankind 2,3,4,59,76,140-141
manner 49,104,113,126,129,149
material enjoyment 14,74
mean 68
meaning of human life 14,74
medicine 1
meddlesome 79
mental illnesses 4

mercy 88
mind, 4,15,35,40,41,44,45,48,73,
76,78,79,85,89,96,97,100,
103,104,122,123,139,141,
144-148,156-160
resistant 5
conduct 8
mischief 122
miserly 70
misunderstanding 57
modern communication tool 59-
62
mood, 80-81,83
bad 80-81,83
moral factors 12
moral sense 4,73
moral value 16
moral view 3
morality 104,121,149
public 149
motivation 54,57
multi-culture inter-blending 4,
156
multi-dimension 4
multi-direction 4
multi-layer 4
mutual consent 128

N

nation 3,140,152,157
national crisis 5
national origin 140-141
nationality 11,140-141
natural objects 47,76,89
narrow-minded 143,158,160
negotiation 96
new conduct 9
new society 4,44,103
nice 69

nicer 16

O

objective 119,120
occupation 11
offend 79
oldster 11
on time 134
open-minded 105
optimism 100
optimistic 92,100,123
order,
social 4
outward appearance 131,132,146
overestimate a friendship 58
overlap, 10,11
partial 10,11
owe 124

P

pain 66,83
painful 66,83
pardon 111
parents 12,51
partial overlap 10,11
particle 158
patient 134
peace, 140-141,157,158,160
mind 85,123
real 140,157,158
peace of mind 85,123
personal freedom 2,3
"personal space" 2,44,45
personality 54
philosophy 1,15
in the narrow sense 15
plane 1
pleasantness 100

pleasure 13,15,43,48,129,135
poverty 147
praise 135
prejudiced words 119
pressure 61
pre-teenager 11,12
pride, 39
    proper 39
privacy 2,44,45
profit 136
promise 37,120
proper behavior 116
proper pride 39
property, 3-4
    complication 4
    contradiction 4
    multi-culture inter-blending 4
    multi-dimension 4
    multi-direction 4
    multi-layer 4
propriety 69
psychological reaction 58,63
    bad 58,63
psychology 1,4
public 149
public morality 149
pure 41

R

race 139
raise 51
rank 11,40,151
rash 89,93
rate, 4
    crimes 4
    drug abuses 4
    mental illnesses 4
    suicide 4

rational 82,95,127,128
rationality 1,95
real friend 112
reasonable 82,96,100
reckless 89
refined behavior 116
region 3,11,142-144,152,157,158,
    160
regret 85,91
relation between conduct and
    health 14-15
relative 13,76,102-104,130
religion choice 148
resolute 106
respect 39,40,44,45,55-56,86,
    97,98,104,125,129,
    139,141,144-148,149
responsibility 76
restraint 82
reward 41,51,77
righteous 41
righteousness 41,77

S

school 5
school lives 13
school security 5
school security actions 5
school violence 5
science 1,3,14,100,120,140
scold 66
security,
    school 5
self-complacent 39
self-confidence 55,79,123
self-constraint 67
self-contained 8
self-control 91

self-examination 109,123
self-respect 55,79,123
self-restraint 82
sensation 54
sense,
    boundaries 160
    honor 50,74
    humor 48
    inferiority 55-56,123
    internationalization 3,140,
        156
    moral 4,73
    public morality 149
    region 158,160
    responsibility 76
    self-confidence 50,55,123
    self-respect 50,55,123
    shame 75
    world 3,140,158
sentiment 1,54,57,142
setback 100
sexual harassment 3,12,151-153
sexual joke 48-49
shame 75
share 135
shift one's responsibility 76
shortsighted 141,143,160
show-off 107
sincere 36,79
sneer 40,48,56,113
social activities 137
social conversation 125,126
social factors 2
social occasion 71,105,116
social order 4
society, 4,76,102-104,157
    constitutional 155
    democratic 155
    healthy 155

human 4,16,156,160
    internationalized 8
    mature 155
    multi-culture inter-blended 8
    new 4,44,103
    old 103
    whole 4,104
society trend 3
sociology 1
soul, 4
    conduct 8
speak ill of others 97
spineless 101
spirit 4,15,77
    conduct 8
spiritual support 2,43
stability 58
state residence 142-144
status 11
steady 89
stingy 68,69,70,129,135
straightforward 102,105
strict 111
strong 101,123
student, 5,8,13
    high-school 8
style, 113
    conversation 113
subjective 119
suicide 4
sympathize 53,138,147
sympathy 47

T

talk reason 81,96
talk recklessly 106,107
teacher 12
tease 48-49,56,113,132

technology 1,3,140
telephone 1,59
temperament 50,54
thanks 133
third person 98
thought 8,14-15
   more mature 15
   wiser 15
thoughtless 68
tip 40
tolerance 61
tolerant 42
tolerate 111,123
toleration 97
tone 113
tools, 1,3,59-62,140,142
   communication 1,3,59-62,
      140,142
      modern 59-62
traffic instruments 1,3,140,142
transfer anger 80,83
trend, 3,102
   society 3,102
trifles 56,89,123
true 35,99
true-hearted 36
trust 56,98,120
trustworthy 120
truth 35

U

underestimate a friendship 58
understand other person (peo-
    ple) 57,86
understand yourself 54,123
united 140,157,158
unity 141
universal harmony 160
universe 158

unpleasant 83
unpleasantness 83,94
unyielding 101,123
upright 41
uprightness 41,112
US (USA) 3,5,6,151-152
US President 5-6,151
US society 151
use a friend 112

V

view,
   a nice human society 160
   dah-turng in the 21st cen-
     tury 160
   moral 3
   peace 157
   sharing the world with all peo-
     ple 160
   the international society 156
   the world 158
   universal harmony 160
violence, 5
   school 5
virtue 51,68,88

W

warm 129
warmth 129
weak 101
wisdom 3,57,140
woman 12,145,151-152
words,
   bad 133
   coarse 113
   dirty 113
   indecent 113
   prejudiced 119

respectful 113
subjective 119
work 2,13
world 5,6,16,42,76,85,94,140,158-
159,160
human 85,129
wonderful 160

Y

yih-chi 77
younger generation 40,79
younger people 40
youth 5,79